Science at the Edge

Genetic Modification of Food

Sally Morgan

D0552852

Heinemann
LIBRARY

www.heinemann.co.uk/library
Visit our website to find out more information about **Heinemann Library** books.

To order:
☎ Phone 44 (0) 1865 888066
🖷 Send a fax to 44 (0) 1865 314091
🖥 Visit the Heinemann Bookshop at www.heinemann.co.uk/library to browse our catalogue and order online.

First published in Great Britain by Heinemann Library, Halley Court, Jordan Hill, Oxford OX2 8EJ, a division of Reed Educational and Professional Publishing Ltd. Heinemann is a registered trademark of Reed Educational and Professional Publishing Ltd.

OXFORD MELBOURNE AUCKLAND JOHANNESBURG BLANTYRE
GABORONE IBADAN PORTSMOUTH NH (USA) CHICAGO

© Reed Educational and Professional Publishing Ltd 2002
The moral right of the proprietor has been asserted.

Designed by Tinstar Design (www.tinstar.co.uk)
Illustrations by Art Construction
Originated by Ambassador Litho Ltd.
Printed and bound in Hong Kong/China

ISBN 0 431 14883 X (hardback)   ISBN 0 431 14890 2 (paperback)
06 05 04 03   06 05 04 03
10 9 8 7 6 5 4 3   10 9 8 7 6 5 4 3 2

British Library Cataloguing in Publication Data
Morgan, Sally
       Genetic modification of food. – (Science at the Edge)
       1. Genetically modified foods – Juvenile literature
       2. Genetically modified foods – Moral and ethical aspects – Juvenile literature
       3. Food – Biotechnology – Juvenile literature
       4. Food – Biotechnology – Moral and ethical aspects – Juvenile literature
       I.Title
       664'.024

Acknowledgements
The Publisher would like to thank the following for permission to reproduce photographs: Corbis: Dan Guravich p49; Ecoscene: pp5, 11 left and right, 12, 31, 51, 53, 54, L. Raman p13; Environmental Images: Pete Addis p55, Graham Bell p50, Martin Bond p35, Vanessa Miles p42, Chris Smith p37; Greenpeace/Lombardi: p39; NHPA: Hellio and van Ingen p23; Oryzabase: p19; Popperfoto/Reuters: pp4, 29; Science Photo Library: pp20, 32, 48, Martin Bond p40, CC Studio p 28, P. Dumas p24, Deborah Ferguson p46, Adam Hart-Davis p44, Chris Knapton p26, Rosenfeld Images Ltd p21; Still Pictures: Nick Cobbing p25, Mark Edwards p56.

Cover photograph reproduced with permission of Science Photo Library.

Our thanks to Dr Michael Winson for his assistance in the preparation of this book.

Any words appearing in the text in bold, **like this**, are explained in the Glossary.

Contents

Introduction

Each year around 600,000 children in the developing world go blind because they do not have enough vitamin A in their diet. Eating a couple of carrots a day would solve the problem, but there are no carrots grown in these countries. Within the next few years these children will be able to eat a special type of rice that has been genetically modified so that it contains enough vitamin A to stop them going blind.

Helping to feed the world

Malnutrition is just one of the challenges in feeding the world's population. At the turn of the Millennium, the human population stood at just over 6 billion. By 2030 there will be 8 billion people, a 30 per cent increase in just 30 years. This massive increase means that governments will have to solve huge problems of hunger and poverty, while also protecting the world's natural environment.

Meeting all of these challenges will require new knowledge gained by scientific advance, and the development of new technologies. Genetic modification or engineering is one of the most promising. It involves changing the genetic content of plants and animals in order to create foodstuffs with new characteristics.

A protest message from the environmental organization Greenpeace in a field of genetically modified soybeans in Iowa, USA.

New crops

Over the last ten years or so, scientists have created a range of new genetically modified (GM) crops. Now, commercial GM crops of soybean, cotton, tobacco, potato and **maize** are grown over millions of hectares in the USA, Canada, China, South Africa and Argentina. These crops are beginning to change the face of agriculture. But this change is not welcomed by everyone. During recent summers, protestors destroyed GM crop trials in both the UK and parts of Europe, and there were protests outside shops selling GM foods. The papers carried scary headlines such as 'Frankenstein foods' and 'Genetic nightmare'. This contributed to a widespread public rejection of genetic modification and the developments linked with it.

In this book you can read about **DNA** and discover how scientists can alter DNA through genetic engineering. You can find out how people can improve crops and livestock through a process called artificial selection, and how this process can be speeded up by using genetic engineering. Many types of genetically altered organisms and foods containing GM products are now sold to the public. Decide for yourself whether GM technology is a good or bad thing and if foods containing GM products are safe to eat.

> *'I have absolutely no anxiety. I am worried by a lot of things, but not about modified food.'*
> Dr James Watson, winner of the Nobel Prize for his work on DNA

A field of GM maize. Each year farmers in the USA plant thousands of hectares of GM crops.

Understanding genes

Every organism carries within it a set of instructions that control all the processes in its cells. The instructions are in the form of codes and they are stored in the **genes**. The genes themselves are made of **DNA** (deoxyribonucleic acid).

Genetic engineering or modification is the deliberate alteration of an organism's genes in order to give it new abilities. For example, bacteria have been given the gene to make the human **protein** insulin. Insulin is a substance that controls the level of glucose in the blood. The term 'genetically modified organism' (GMO) is used to describe a plant, animal or micro-organism that has had its DNA altered in some way by genetic engineering.

Early genetics

Our understanding of genetics dates back to the time of Gregor Mendel, who carried out experiments using peas during the 1860s. In one experiment he crossed tall peas with dwarf peas and found that all the offspring were tall. He concluded that the features of the two parents were not blended together to produce medium height peas. Instead the feature of one parent, in this case the tall parent, would appear in the offspring, while the other feature did not appear – it was masked.

Mendel's work forms the basis of modern genetics. It is important to remember that he discovered the laws of inheritance without any knowledge of cell structure or biochemistry. It was only at the beginning of the 20th century, when more powerful microscopes were invented, that biologists were able to study the genetic material found in the **nucleus** – the **chromosomes**. It wasn't until the 1920s that the substance that makes up the chromosomes – DNA – was discovered.

DNA structure

However, the major breakthrough in the understanding of genetics came in 1953, when Francis Crick and James Watson, with help from Rosalind Franklin, determined the structure of the DNA **molecule**. Since then, our knowledge of DNA and the **genetic code** has improved dramatically. This knowledge has enabled scientists to alter DNA and to transfer it between organisms.

DNA is a long molecule that consists of two strands twisted around each other to form a spiral called a helix. It can be likened to a twisted ladder: the sides of the ladder are made from alternating sugar and phosphate molecules, and the rungs are formed by molecules called bases. There are four different bases in DNA – adenine (A), guanine (G), cytosine (C) and thymine (T). A and G are large molecules, while C and T molecules are smaller ones. Each rung consists of one large molecule joined to a small one so that the width is always the same. In addition, A always pairs with T, and C with G. It is the order of bases along a strand of DNA that forms the genetic code.

Discovering the double helix

Probably the most exciting and significant biological discovery of the 20th century was solving the structure of DNA. In 1953, Francis Crick and James Watson published the details of their proposed structure of DNA. It had been known for some time that DNA was made up of sugar, phosphate and the four bases – adenine, guanine, cytosine and thymine – but nobody knew how these components were joined together. One of the vital parts of the puzzle was provided by Edwin Chargaff. During the late 1940s his research had found that the number of guanine bases equalled the number of cytosine bases and, similarly, the number of adenine bases equalled the number of thymine bases. Then, Maurice Wilkins and Rosalind Franklin took an 'X-ray' of the DNA, which showed that it formed a helix. Finally, Crick and Watson studied all the evidence and decided that DNA in fact formed a double helix.

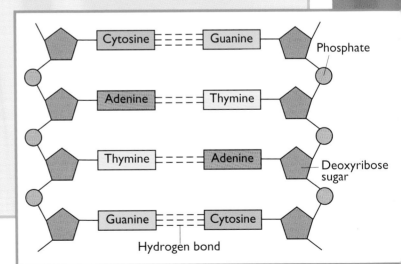

DNA is made up of sugar and phosphate molecules together with four different types of bases. The two strands of the DNA are held together by weak bonds called hydrogen bonds.

Genes and simple genetics

Genes control the manufacture of proteins in the cell. There are thousands of different genes, each responsible for making a specific protein. In a human cell there are two copies of each gene, one inherited from the father and the other from the mother. Genes can exist in two forms. One form is described as being dominant and the other as being recessive. The dominant form of the gene will usually mask the appearance of the recessive form. A person can have two dominant genes, one dominant and one recessive, or two recessive.

For example, humans can have brown eyes or blue eyes. The dominant gene codes for brown pigment in eyes and the recessive form codes for blue eyes. To have brown eyes, a person must inherit at least one gene for brown eyes. This means that both of the genes could be brown or just one. The outward appearance is always the same – brown eyes. To have blue eyes a person must have two blue-eye genes – in other words, they have to have inherited a blue-eye gene from each parent. This is a very simplified explanation of inheritance. In reality, most characteristics are controlled by several genes working together.

Inheriting genes

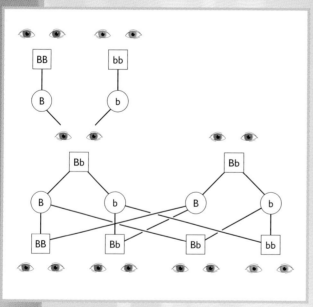

In this diagram, the letter B represents the gene for brown eyes and b represents the gene for blue eyes. (Remember a person inherits one gene from each parent.) If a brown-eyed person (BB) with two brown-eye genes mates with a person with blue eyes (bb), all the children will have brown eyes. They have one brown-eye gene and one blue-eye gene (Bb). The blue-eye gene is masked by the brown-eye gene. If one of these children mates with a person with the same genes, there are three possible outcomes. Three out of four children will have brown eyes (BB and Bb). One out of four will have blue eyes.

Recombinant DNA

In 1970, researchers discovered **enzymes** that could cut the DNA at specific points. These enzymes were essential to the process of cutting out a length of DNA and pasting it into the DNA of another organism. This created **recombinant DNA** – DNA made up of one or more lengths from different organisms. The first successful transfer of DNA took place in 1973. During the 1980s, the first **transgenic** animals and plants appeared. These were organisms that contained genetic material that had been artificially inserted from another species.

During the 1990s a wide range of genetically modified animals and plants were produced, followed by the appearance of GM foods in shops. It was at this stage that the first concerns about the genetic modification of foods started to appear in the media.

Key players

Genetically modified plants and animals are produced by a wide range of international **biotechnology** companies and research institutes. Before a GMO may be used commercially, it has to be approved by the food agencies of the various governments, for example the Advisory Committee on Novel Foods and Processes in the UK. In addition, international organizations such as the Food and Agriculture Organization (FAO) and the Codex Alimentarius Commission provide advice and guidance to governments and help to draw up internationally agreed standards.

Food and Agriculture Organization (FAO)

The FAO was established in 1945 as an independent organization of the **United Nations**. Its role is to promote agricultural development and to improve the nutritional standards of rural populations. It aims to provide all people with access at all times to the food they require for an active and healthy life. It offers direct development assistance; collects, analyses and distributes information; provides policy and planning advice to governments; and acts as an international forum for debate on food and agricultural issues. In 1999, a task force was set up to investigate the safety of GM food, and in 2001 it published a draft document called 'General principles for risk analysis of foods derived from biotechnology'. Risk analysis is the system by which governments consider the safety of foods and the measures that need to be taken to protect the public from any health risk.

Improving plants and animals

Plant and animal breeding has produced higher yield crops, plants with better pest and disease **resistance**, larger meat animals and dairy cows that produce thousands of litres of milk per year.

First farmers

Twenty thousand years ago or more, people were hunter-gatherers. They moved from place to place, hunting animals and collecting fruits and nuts from the wild. Then people settled down and started to grow their own crops. They sowed seed collected from wild grasses and at the end of the growing season they harvested the seeds. They soon learnt to save the seed from the plants that gave the best yield as this would produce a better crop. As a result of this selection process, the yield of the first cereal crops increased greatly.

The story of wheat

Wheat can be traced back to wild grasses that were growing thousands of years ago. These grasses had cells that contained 14 **chromosomes**. The different types of wild grasses were grown together and, by chance, a **hybrid** plant was produced. This grass had 28 chromosomes, double the original number. It was a far more vigorous plant and had larger seeds. Thousands of years later another lucky crossing produced the modern wheat plant, which has 42 chromosomes. Recently, a new cereal called Triticale has been produced by cross-breeding durum wheat (*Triticum*) with rye (*Secale*). Triticale is a versatile cereal with good yield and hardiness so it can be grown in harsh climates.

Natural selection vs artificial selection

Natural selection is one of the processes by which evolution occurs. In any group of individuals of the same species there will be a few that are better suited to the environment than others. The best adapted individuals survive and breed, passing on their **genes** to their offspring. This is often called 'survival of the fittest'.

Imagine several plants, from the same species, that have prickly leaves. The individual plants that have more prickly leaves are less likely to be eaten by grazing animals than those which have just a few prickles. So more prickly plants survive and produce seeds that grow into plants that also have more prickles. Over time, the less prickly plants disappear and the more prickly ones increase.

Farmers have replaced natural selection with artificial selection, that is selection based on a human decision. If this species of plant was good to eat, it is easy to imagine that the farmer would have chosen to grow the less prickly plants. It wouldn't matter that the plants were more vulnerable to grazing animals because the animals would have been kept out by fences. Gradually, the plants become less prickly. In effect, the farmer has selected certain genes.

A similar process has occurred with animals. The first animals to be domesticated were herd animals, that could be rounded up and kept in corrals (fenced-off areas). The early farmers bred from the smaller animals that were easier to handle and did not eat as much as the larger ones. Today, domesticated animals are bred for size, muscle and milk production.

Most calves are raised for beef, so farmers often cross a beef-type bull, such as the Hereford (right), with more docile dairy Friesians (left) to produce a calf that is good for beef and easy to handle.

Characteristics of artificial selection

Speed and success rates

The process of artificial selection is slow, especially with animals. Larger animals take several years to mature and only produce one offspring at a time. The process is also pretty hit and miss. Farmers choose the parents with care, trying to bring together animals with desirable features, for example a ewe and a ram that both have good quality wool. But there is no guarantee that two sheep with quality wool will produce offspring with even better quality wool. Sometimes the new combination of features in the offspring can actually make it worse, rather than better.

Changes can be seen more quickly in plants. First, the parent plants with the desirable characteristics are identified. Pollen is removed from the flowers of one plant and used to **pollinate** the flowers on another. Since plants generally produce many seeds, all the seeds are **germinated** and the new plants examined to see if there has been any improvement.

Mutations

Sometimes, a completely new variation appears in the genetic material of the offspring. These sudden changes are called mutations. Many mutations are harmful to the organism and it does not survive, but occasionally they are useful and the animal or plant passes on the mutation to their offspring. Some mutations have been known to greatly improve a crop plant or an animal.

A high yielding variety of wheat has a short stalk that is less susceptible to lodging (bending over after wind and rain). It also produces an 'ear' or seed head with many seeds that swell in size and ripen ready for harvest at the same time.

For example, in wild grasses the seed stalk shatters easily in order to disperse the seeds. Early in the history of wheat, a **mutant** appeared that had a strong seed stalk. This was a real bonus to farmers, as the seeds stayed attached to the plant and could be collected. This mutation would have been disastrous in a wild grass as the plant would have been unable to spread its seeds.

Recent developments

Breeders continue to use **selective breeding** programmes to improve crops and livestock. Recently, researchers crossed a commercial Chinese variety of rice with a bizarre-looking wild rice and boosted the rice yield by a staggering 10 to 20 per cent. Similarly, there is a new variety of oil-seed rape (an oil-producing crop that has yellow flowers) called smart canola, that has natural resistance to two herbicides. It was created by crossing plants that each had resistance to a different herbicide. Now the farmer can spray the crop with two different herbicides, killing a greater range of weeds without harming the crop.

> 'If you do it [crop breeding] by natural methods, we have no problem with that. This could be extremely effective, and you don't need to get genes from daffodils or micro-organisms.'
>
> Benedikt Haerlin, spokesperson on genetic engineering for the environmental organization Greenpeace

It is important to maintain as many different varieties of rice as possible in case they are useful in plant breeding programmes. Research at this centre in Hyderabad, India, is studying the resistance of different rice varieties to the white backed plant hopper, a major insect pest.

Genetic changes

Traditional **selective breeding** methods are based on the transfer of genetic material between individuals of the same species. Some genetic engineering is not that different to selective breeding, but it is a far more rapid and precise process. However, genetic engineering also makes it possible to move **genes** between species that would not normally interbreed – something that cannot usually be achieved using selective breeding.

Transgenic organisms

Plants and animals that contain foreign **DNA** are called **transgenics**. For example, sheep that have been given an extra gene to make a substance that is normally made by humans are transgenic because they contain human DNA. The change in the sheep's DNA means that it is different from other animals of the same type – it is a new strain.

Organisms that receive a new gene have new abilities. They may be able to make a new **protein** or **enzyme**, or produce a substance such as an **antibiotic**. It is this feature that makes the technique of genetic engineering revolutionary, in terms of the potential benefits it can bring.

Genetic engineering has the following advantages over traditional selective breeding:
- the desired change can be achieved in very few generations
- it is faster and lower in cost
- it allows greater precision in selecting characteristics
- it allows a much wider selection of traits for improvement. In plants, for example, it can introduce pest, disease, drought and herbicide **resistance** as well as improved nutritional content.

Making proteins

Proteins are essential building blocks and have many functions in the body. Haemoglobin, for example, is the oxygen-carrying substance in the blood. Keratin in the skin, nails and hair is a structural protein.

Each gene is responsible for the manufacture of a specific protein. For example, one gene carries the instructions for a specific type of blood protein, while another is responsible for making the brown pigment found in skin, hair and eyes. All proteins are made from **amino acids**. There are 20 different amino acids, and it is the composition of these and the order in which they occur within the protein that determines the type of protein.

If a gene mutates in some way, the **genetic code** may be changed. This means that cells may not be able to make a particular protein and the body suffers from a malfunction. A single faulty gene, for example, causes the disease cystic fibrosis, which affects the lungs and digestive system.

Protein synthesis

Part of a DNA **molecule** in the **nucleus** unwinds to expose the bases. The genetic code is formed from groups of three bases. Each group of three bases identifies a specific amino acid. There are 64 possible combinations of the four bases – A, T, G and C. As there are only 20 amino acids, some amino acids have more than one code while others are used to indicate the start and finish of the message.

A messenger molecule (**RNA**) is used to carry the information from the DNA in the nucleus to the **cytoplasm**. Here, the RNA attaches to a tiny structure called a ribosome and the code is read, one group of three bases at a time. The corresponding amino acids are picked up from the cytoplasm and joined together in the correct order. This forms a strand of amino acids that makes up new protein.

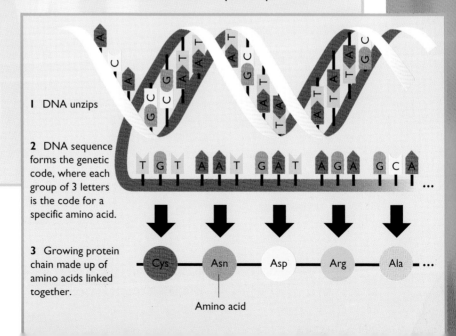

1 DNA unzips

2 DNA sequence forms the genetic code, where each group of 3 letters is the code for a specific amino acid.

3 Growing protein chain made up of amino acids linked together.

Amino acid

Genetic engineering – the process

The first stage in genetic engineering is to identify the desired gene on the DNA of the donor organism. Once located, the gene has to be 'cut out' and then 'pasted' into another piece of DNA which will be inserted into the recipient organism. DNA that contains foreign DNA is referred to as **recombinant DNA**.

Molecular scissors

Scientists use special enzymes to chop up DNA into many small pieces. These enzymes act like molecular scissors. There are thousands of different special enzymes, each of which cuts at a specific point on the DNA. These enzymes make it easier to find and remove individual genes. Now it is possible to remove a specific length of DNA from one organism and insert it into the DNA of another. Before the selected length of DNA can be pasted into the new DNA, it has to be copied billions of times to produce enough material to work with. This takes place in a solution containing a specific mix of chemicals.

Inserting the DNA

Once the length of DNA has been copied it has to be inserted into the host cell. Some animal cells can be persuaded to take up new DNA by simply injecting it into their nucleus. First, the new DNA is attached to a length of DNA that has been taken from the animal cell, so the cell will recognize it. Then the new DNA and the bit to which it is attached get stitched into the host cell's own DNA.

In bacteria, a circular piece of DNA called a plasmid, found in the cytoplasm, is used to get the DNA into the host bacterium. The desired gene is first stitched into the plasmid and then the plasmid is inserted into the bacterium.

The cells of plants, however, are surrounded by a thick cell wall. In order to introduce the new DNA, some plants are genetically modified using natural plant parasites. One type of soil bacterium, for example, has a natural ability to transfer its own genes into a plant – 'nature's own genetic engineer'. This ability is used by geneticists (scientists who study genetics) to insert other genes of interest. Cereals are genetically modified using a gene gun. The gun fires tungsten (a type of metal) particles coated in DNA at the plant. The particles penetrate the plant cell wall and some enter the nucleus where the foreign DNA becomes incorporated into the cell's own DNA. A bizarre method that works!

Genetically engineered chymosin

Cheese is traditionally made using rennet. Rennet is essential to cheese-making as it curdles the milk, separating it into solid curds and liquid whey. The curds are pressed to make cheese. Natural rennet is obtained from the stomachs of young calves – the rennet contains an enzyme that enables the animal to digest milk. However, because rennet is taken from animals, many people, including vegetarians, do not eat traditionally manufactured cheese. Now an artificial rennet containing chymosin is manufactured using genetically modified yeast.

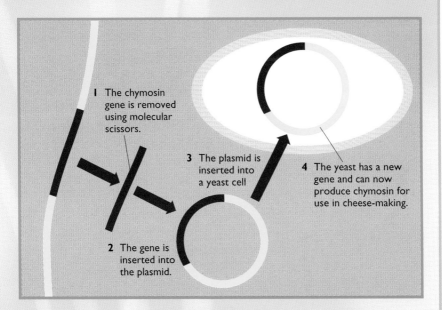

1 The chymosin gene is removed using molecular scissors.

2 The gene is inserted into the plasmid.

3 The plasmid is inserted into a yeast cell

4 The yeast has a new gene and can now produce chymosin for use in cheese-making.

The scientists who developed the artificial rennet located the gene for chymosin on cow's DNA and removed it using specific molecular scissors. The DNA was cut in such a way that one strand of DNA was left longer than the other, creating what is called a 'sticky end'. A plasmid was cut open and the new DNA added to one end. The ends were rejoined using another enzyme. This technique is called gene splicing. The engineered plasmid was then inserted into a yeast cell, giving the yeast the ability to make chymosin. The plasmid remains within the yeast and each time the yeast reproduces, the chymosin gene is passed on to a new generation of yeast.

Despite the fact that chymosin is a product of GM yeast, many vegetarian societies consider it a preferable source of rennet. Today chymosin makes up more than half of the world's supply of rennet. However, adverse publicity concerning GM foods during the late 1990s led to cheese manufacturers seeking an alternative. A yeast has now been discovered that produces a chymosin-like substance naturally.

Expressing itself

Once inside the cell, the next problem is to get the gene to work or to express itself. For example, if a geneticist has inserted a gene for producing a particular protein in the seeds, they do not want the plant producing the protein in its leaves. **Chromosomes** have control regions that switch certain genes on or off. So as well as being able to successfully insert a new gene, the geneticist has to be able to alter the control region so that the new gene is switched on in the places where it is required.

Genetic markers

Once DNA has been inserted into the DNA of another organism, the researchers need to prove that the process has been successful. This is achieved using marker genes, which are attached to the target gene. One of the most common markers is a gene that makes the new organism resistant to a specific antibiotic. To check that bacteria, for example, have been successfully modified, they are spread on to a plate of agar jelly which contains the antibiotic ampicillin. The ampicillin will normally kill all the bacteria. Only those bacteria which contain the genetic marker gene will be able to grow and reproduce. These cells can be isolated and cultured to produce more bacteria. The bacteria are then modified again to remove the marker gene. Some of the early GM **maize** plants also contained a marker gene that gave resistance to ampicillin. If the plant showed resistance to ampicillin, it also contained the gene for resistance to a pest called the corn borer mite.

There are other types of genetic marker. A type of jellyfish exists that glows green in the dark. The gene which causes this has been identified and removed. It can be attached to other genes and inserted into a different organism. In this case scientists can tell the modification has been successful when the organism glows green!

'Understanding cereal genetic structure and associated proteins will enable plant breeders to produce crops that are more nutritious, more productive and easier to process. We will also research new ways to protect crops from diseases or pests and discover new uses for crop plants. This offers exciting new opportunities to improve agricultural yields and quality.'

Dr David Evans, Head of Research and Technology at Syngenta

The rice genome

In January 2001, the **biotechnology** company Syngenta announced that it had completed the rice **genome** map. Their researchers had determined the complete DNA sequence – the exact order of bases (cytosine, guanine, thymine and adenine) – along a DNA strand in rice, as well as identifying some of the sequences that control gene activity and the location of most of the genes. A more detailed analysis of gene activity and function and the resulting proteins is underway. Rice has 12 chromosomes and 50,000 genes. This adds up to 430 million base pairs on the DNA. Rice is very similar to other cereals so the information gained from rice will contribute to the study of other important cereals such as wheat, corn and barley, and lead to their future improvement. Rice is a vital crop in the developing world and Syngenta promises that it will work with local research institutes to explore how this information can best be used to find crop improvements to benefit **subsistence farmers**.

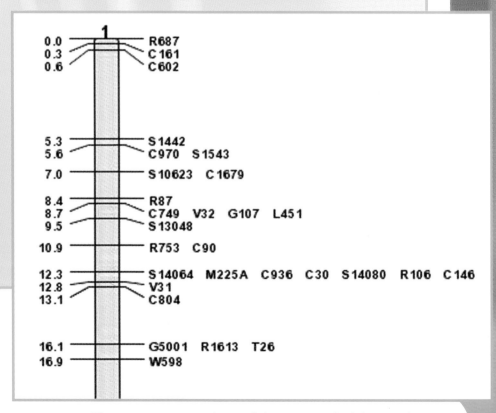

This is a genetic map of part of chromosome 1 of the rice plant. The lines show the position and name of the genes as they occur along the DNA. Chromosome 1 is the largest of the 12 chromosomes and is expected to have about 7000 genes.

Cloning

Successfully modifying the DNA of an organism takes time and luck. Then scientists have to find ways of producing more without altering the DNA again. They need exact copies or **clones**. Bacteria and yeast increase in number by simply dividing into two. The new cell is an exact copy of the parent cell. Therefore, genetically modified bacteria and yeast are easy to reproduce as the DNA remains the same.

Genetically modified plants have to be **propagated** asexually using cuttings or tissue culture. For example, a length of shoot can be taken from a plant and treated in such a way that it grows roots. The new plant is identical to the parent. Or plants can be reproduced from tiny samples of tissue. The sample is placed in a **growth medium**, which causes the cells to grow shoots and roots. Seeds cannot be used as they are produced by sexual reproduction. Pollen from one plant **pollinates** a flower on another plant, which then develops seeds. The seeds contain genes from both parents, which means that the resulting plants will be different to both parents.

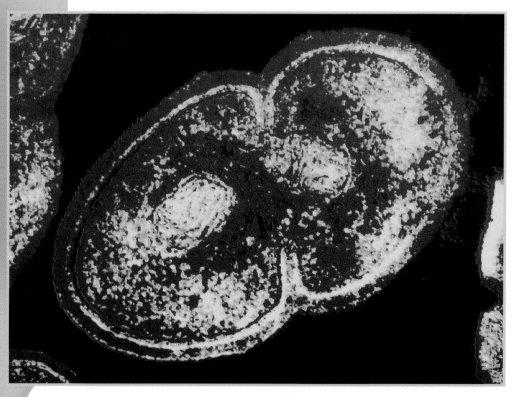

Organisms such as bacteria and yeast reproduce by simply dividing into two. This is called binary fission. The two new cells are identical to each other.

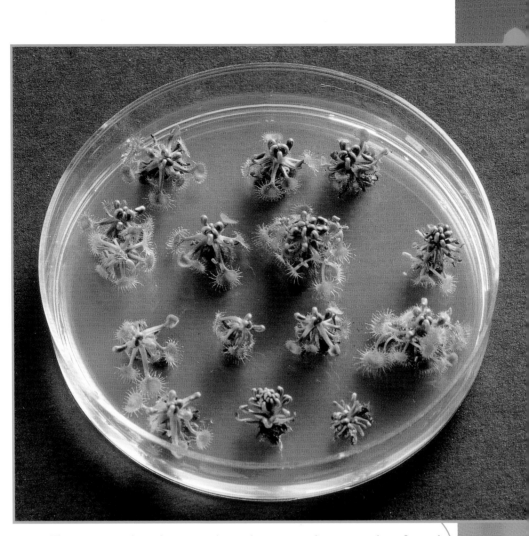

These tiny sundew plants are identical copies to the parent plant. Several samples of cells were taken from the parent and placed on the growth medium. This contains carefully controlled quantities of plant growth substances, which cause new shoots and roots to form.

Mammals are far more complex and difficult to clone. However, the cloning of animals does occur naturally – for example, identical twins are clones of each other. The **fertilized** egg splits in two and two **embryos** develop instead of one. Each embryo has the same genetic composition. Currently, the most common way of cloning a mammal artificially is to take an egg cell, remove its nucleus and replace it with a nucleus taken from a genetically modified mammal. The egg is treated so that it divides and develops into a new individual (see page 28).

New crops

During the last ten years or so a range of GM crops has become available. Many of these crops are either being grown in North and South America and China, or are undergoing trials in Europe.

As we have seen in the previous chapter, genetic engineering offers a number of advantages over traditional **selective breeding**. These advantages could, in turn, lead to a number of benefits:
- better yields while using fewer pesticides
- an ability to grow crops in previously inhospitable environments, because of increased ability of plants to grow in conditions of drought, salinity (saltiness) and extremes of temperature
- improved sensory attributes of food – for example, flavour and texture
- better nutritional content – for example, increased Vitamin A content in rice, or removal of the factors that cause **allergies** to certain foods such as nuts
- easier processing that leads to reduced waste and lower food costs to the consumer.

Pesticides

Pests can devastate crops. They eat plant leaves, reducing crop yield and quality. In all parts of the world, pests can be incredibly damaging. Locusts, for example, can consume a whole crop in just a few hours. As a result, farmers have to protect their crops by using pesticides. Most pesticides are chemicals that kill either a specific pest or a range of pests. Insecticides are used to kill insect pests and fungicides are used on fungal pests. Herbicides kill unwanted plants or weeds. Some herbicides such as glyphosate and paraquat kill all plants with which they come into contact. Others just kill plants with narrow leaves such as grasses, or plants with broad leaves – dock and thistles, for example.

Pesticides have some advantages. They are quick acting, generally reliable and can be applied with ease. But there are disadvantages. They are expensive to buy and require the use of specialized equipment. Many pesticides kill insects indiscriminately, destroying useful as well as harmful insects. For example, some pesticides kill both the greenfly and its natural predator, the ladybird. Most modern pesticides are designed to break down once they have been in the soil for a few weeks, so that they do not remain in the environment. However, heavy rainfall shortly after spraying can wash off the pesticide, forcing the farmer to re-spray. The run-off can drain into streams, rivers and lakes where the pesticides harm aquatic life. Pesticides don't kill all of the pests so they usually have to be reapplied. For example, in the southern USA, cotton may be sprayed up to eight times a year and still up to fifteen per cent of the crop may be lost to pests. Finally, there are fears that residue from pesticides that remains on food crops may harm the health of consumers.

Pests such as locusts strip plants of all their leaves. They can destroy whole fields of crop plants in just a few hours. This can cause food shortages for the people living in the region.

Pesticide resistance

Among the first genetically engineered plants were those that had been given built-in **resistance** to pests. One **gene** of particular interest is found in the soil bacterium, *Bacillus thuringiensis*, known as Bt. This bacterium produces a selective **toxin** that is poisonous to most insects, especially caterpillars, but harmless to most other organisms. An organic insecticide can be made by growing the bacteria and then drying them to form a powder containing the poison. But the powder is difficult to use and not always effective. The gene that makes the toxin was identified, removed and inserted into crop plants such as **maize**, cabbage and cotton. Cotton plants have been given this gene so that they can produce the toxin to kill the cotton boll worm. These cotton varieties are grown widely in the USA, where bumper harvests have been reported and costs are down. In 2001, GM cotton made up 64 per cent of the total US cotton crop.

A scientist monitors the uptake of oxygen by a melon plant. The melons have been modified so that they ripen more slowly, giving them a longer shelf life.

Stay-fresh vegetables

As well as giving crops resistance to disease and pests, some of the modifications are aimed at improving the shelf life of vegetables, especially salad vegetables. These vegetables spoil quickly on the shelves, creating a lot of waste. One way to increase the shelf life is to slow down the ripening process, so producers have more time to get their vegetables to market. The ripening process involves an **enzyme** called pectinase. This enzyme breaks down the pectin that holds plant cells together. When this happens, the fruit or vegetable softens. Researchers have targeted this enzyme in the tomato. They removed the gene and replaced it 'back-to-front'. This simple procedure switched off the gene and prevented the enzyme from being made. The altered tomatoes ripened more slowly. They remained firm for much longer, were easier to handle and there was much less waste.

Crop trials

Although GM crops are widely planted in North America, they are still undergoing testing and evaluation in the UK. Three GM crops are undergoing field trials – GM maize, oil-seed rape and sugar beet. The trials are designed to investigate the effect of the GM crop on local wildlife and to monitor the spread of pollen. Once the results of the three-year trials are known, the UK government will make a decision on whether these crops can be grown commercially. Specific fields are designated as trial sites. These fields are chosen with care to make sure they are not too close to non-GM crops being grown in the same area (this is explained more fully on page 50). The trial crop is surrounded by a barrier crop of a non-GM variety. During the growing season, scientists check the plants and monitor the wildlife. At the end of the growing season the crop is harvested and destroyed. Unfortunately a large number of field trials in the UK have been destroyed by protestors, so the research has been incomplete.

PRIVATE LAND
GMO TRIAL
KEEP OFF

The GM oil-seed rape growing in this field is part of a three-year field trial which is studying the effect of growing GM crops on local wildlife.

Herbicide resistance

Glyphosate is a widely used and relatively cheap, non-selective herbicide. It kills most of the plants with which it comes into contact, but it does not persist in the soil. As a garden weedkiller it is ideal, but it cannot be used on crops because it would kill them. Now there are GM crops that have a gene from a bacterium that gives them resistance to glyphosate, for example glyphosate-resistant soybean. Soybean is grown widely in the USA and Brazil. It is an important source of **protein** and is used in processed food and animal feeds. Before the arrival of this GM soybean, farmers could only use selective herbicides, which were expensive and often persisted in the ground for many months. Now they can use the cheaper and more environmentally-friendly glyphosate. The glyphosate-resistant soybean is just one of several herbicide-resistant crop plants. Varieties of maize, sugar beet and oil-seed rape have all been modified to give them resistance to certain types of herbicide.

Weeds growing amongst crop plants compete with them for water, nutrients and space. If they are not removed the crop yield will be reduced. Now it is possible to spray GM maize plants with the weedkiller glyphosate to kill all the weeds without harming the crop. The dead weeds form a layer over the soil that traps moisture, helping the crop.

New crops on the way

In the USA, there is a wide variety of GM foods either approved for sale or awaiting approval. These include apples, asparagus, barley, beetroot, carrots, cauliflower, grapes, kiwi, lettuce, maize, melons, papaya, peanuts, peppers, potatoes, strawberries, rice, soya, sugarcane, tomatoes and wheat. Not all of these foods may be sold in the European Union (EU), as they have not completed the approval process. So far, the EU has approved GM maize and soya, and GM tomato for use in processed foods.

The following table shows some of the crops with new characteristics that are currently undergoing field trials around the world.

Crop	Improved feature
Apple	Insect resistance
Banana	Plants that are free of viruses and worm parasites
Broccoli	Slower ripening, so flower head stays green for longer and doesn't turn yellow
Cabbage	Resistance to attack by caterpillars
Celery	Retention of crispness
Coffee	Better flavour, yields and pest resistance; lower caffeine content
Cucumber	Resistance to viruses, fungi and bacteria
Melon	Extended shelf life
Potato	Resistance to caterpillars and beetles; lower **fertilizer** requirement; lower water content so less fat is absorbed in cooking process (low-fat chips)
Raspberry	Increased sugar content; extended shelf life
Strawberry	Frost resistance, allowing early season production
Sunflower	More nutritious oils with lower saturated fat content
Tomato	Resistance to viral diseases; increased yield; slower ripening; resistance to rotting after harvest; lower water content; frost resistance; increased sugar content
Wheat	Flour more suitable for bread-making; resistance to herbicide

The GM crop producers

Over the last ten years, there has been a lot of change in the plant science field. The number of companies involved in crop research has fallen, but those companies that remain are huge multinational corporations with global interests. The reason for these changes is the increasing costs of crop development, especially in the field of **biotechnology**. The major players include Monsanto, AgrEvo, Aventis and DuPont. These companies have invested millions of pounds in the development of the first generation of GM crops, including a maize that produces a pesticide, a soybean that is resistant to herbicides and a tomato that has a longer shelf life.

Genetically modified animals

Animals have also been genetically altered to improve their performance, although there are fewer examples compared with plants and they are far less easy to produce.

The modification process

Genetically modifying an animal such as a fish, bird or mammal is far more complex than modifying bacteria or plants. The animal has to be altered while it is at the **embryo** stage. After **fertilization**, the new cell starts to divide and within a few days it is a ball of cells. To ensure that all the cells contain the new **DNA**, the fertilized egg has to be altered before it divides. A length of DNA is removed from the donor organism and injected into the **nucleus** of the egg. Then it may or may not become incorporated into the DNA. The procedure is a bit hit and miss – often it has to be carried out on hundreds of fertilized egg cells just to be successful with one or two.

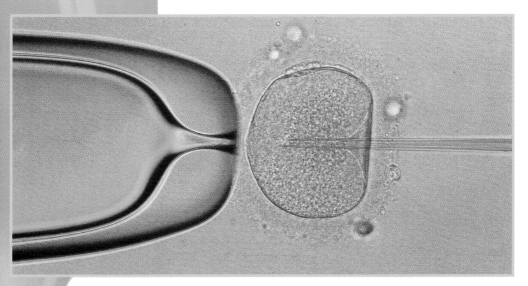

New DNA has to be inserted into a newly fertilized egg before it starts to divide. The DNA to be inserted is taken up by a micropipette and then injected into the nucleus of the egg.

The first experiments on mice

The first experiments aimed at producing genetically engineered animals were carried out on mice. Scientists injected some DNA into the nucleus of a fertilized egg, and this DNA joined to one of the **chromosomes** to become a permanent part of the mouse's genetic make-up. The DNA contained a gene that enabled the mouse to grow much larger than normal. The altered egg was placed back inside the uterus of a female mouse and allowed to develop naturally. The mouse gave birth to a youngster that contained the new gene, and it therefore grew to be much larger than normal.

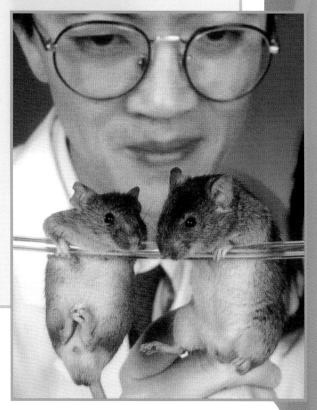

The mouse on the right has been genetically altered so that it does not suffer from the weakening of muscles that usually occurs in old age. Information gained from these experiments will help research into the disease muscular dystrophy.

Improving animals

Research is underway to genetically alter pigs, cattle, chickens, sheep and fish. There are many potential benefits of GM animals. These include better growth rates, leaner meat and disease **resistance**. Researchers in Israel are aiming to produce a featherless chicken while researchers in the UK are hoping to produce grass-eating pigs and chickens. In the future, it could be possible to produce animals that are resistant to diseases such as foot-and-mouth. However, there have been some unpleasant results. A pig that had been modified with a human growth hormone grew bigger and more quickly than usual. But it suffered from arthritis (swollen joints), developed ulcers and was sterile.

Super salmon

Salmon will probably be the first genetically modified animals to be released commercially. These salmon have had **genes** from a flounder (type of flat fish) inserted into their DNA. The new genes increase the salmon's growth rate by between 400 and 600 per cent. Also, the fish have a slightly lower fat content which would benefit the health of consumers. The altered salmon do not grow any larger than normal salmon, but they reach full size much quicker. For example, at 18 months, the salmon are five times the size of unmodified salmon of the same age. This means that the GM salmon will be ready for harvest in 16–18 months compared with three years. This development could cut the costs of rearing salmon by half and allow a more rapid production cycle.

The Canadian company that has produced the salmon claims that all the salmon are infertile. However, organizations that are campaigning against the release of the salmon, such as the Royal Societies of Canada and the UK, say that it is impossible to guarantee sterility. They are concerned that the modified salmon will escape from fish farms and interbreed with wild salmon, allowing the gene for faster growth to spread through the wild populations. One way forward would be to allow the commercial production of the salmon, but to make it compulsory to keep the fish in land-locked pens. This way there would be no risk of the salmon escaping. Another problem that has emerged is the fact that some of the salmon are deformed. This is probably a result of the fish growing so quickly.

Although salmon is the first to be altered, many other types of commercial fish could be modified in the future, including trout, tilipia and Arctic char. Tilipia is an important source of **protein** in many parts of the world. The ability to produce more fish in less time could help to alleviate food shortages in some of the poorest countries of the world.

> 'While we acknowledge that some applications of the technology may bring benefits, we are concerned that GM animals may be produced simply because it is possible, and not because it is necessary. This is unacceptable.'
> Spokesperson from the Royal Society for the Prevention of Cruelty to Animals, commenting on the increasing numbers of scientific procedures involving GM animals – up by 63,000 between 1998 and 1999 to a total of 511,000

More milk

Mammals produce a growth hormone that affects the rate at which they grow and produce muscles. This hormone is called bovine somatotrophin in cattle. Farmers found that when they injected dairy cows with extra bovine somatotrophin, or BST, the cows produced more milk and muscle. Originally the BST was taken from dead cows, but it can now be produced from genetically modified bacteria. It is called rBST (recombinant bovine somatotrophin) to distinguish it from the naturally produced hormone. A single dose of BST every two weeks can boost the milk yield of a cow by as much as 25 per cent. However there is a downside. So much energy is directed into producing milk, that the animal is more likely to become ill. Cows receiving the treatment are more susceptible to udder infections, gut problems and they often become lame. This means that the cow has to be given **antibiotics** and other medicines. It may even shorten her productive life.

The milk yield of every cow passing through a dairy parlour is monitored and her diet altered accordingly. This way, the diet can be optimized for maximum milk production. Injections of rBST could increase milk yield further still.

Cloning animals

At the moment, the only way to produce new **transgenic** animals is to alter the DNA of normal embryos. This is an expensive procedure, so transgenic animals are very valuable. The next stage is to develop the procedure to **clone** these valuable animals. Clones are exact genetic copies of the original individual. They are rather like identical twins. Identical twins result when a fertilized egg splits into two, and each of the cells grows into a new individual. The genetic material in each of the individuals is the same, hence they are clones.

In 1996, Dolly the sheep was born. Her birth represented a very important milestone in the field of genetics, as she was the first clone of an adult mammalian cell. The procedure involved taking an udder cell from an adult ewe. The nucleus was removed from the udder cell and placed inside an empty egg cell that had been taken from another ewe. The egg cell was treated so that it started to divide to produce an embryo. This embryo was placed inside the uterus of another sheep who actually gave birth to Dolly. Dolly was a clone of the ewe who had donated the udder cell.

Many people are concerned that clones such as Dolly the sheep may not be as healthy as normal animals and that they may have short lifespans. In 2002, it was discovered that Dolly had developed arthritis. However, it was not known whether or not this was caused by the process of cloning.

This procedure proved that it was possible to clone mammals such as sheep, although hundreds of unsuccessful attempts were made before Dolly was produced. Since then clones of goats and cows have been produced.

Cloned dairy cows

In 2001, a **biotechnology** company produced healthy clones of a top dairy cow. Zita was a top ranking Holstein dairy cow in the USA. Her daughters were also top ranking cows, producing much more milk than other Holsteins. However, every time one of these top cows was mated with a bull, there was a chance that the offspring would not be so productive as their mother. The only way to ensure that all the future generations would be equally productive was to clone Zita. Cells were taken from Zita before she died and used to produce clones.

However, at present, the success rate is low and many clones are born with abnormalities or they die shortly after birth. In time the technique will improve and it may become a relatively easy process to produce clones of top ranking cows, bulls and genetically modified animals.

Are we playing at being God?

Some people feel that scientists are 'playing at being God' when they alter animals. They consider that genetically modifying animals so that they can make drugs or produce more food turns them into instruments or 'living drugs factories'. They find this ethically unacceptable. However, it is important to remember that people have been changing animals ever since they were first domesticated. Modern breeds of livestock and pets are very different from the original wild species. They are kept under conditions very different to those experienced in the wild, and if released, they would probably not survive since they have become so dependent on people for food. Genetic engineering is similar to **selective breeding**, except, of course, that it can be achieved more quickly.

There is also concern over the welfare of transgenic animals. However, the fact that an animal is transgenic does not itself create welfare problems. Rather it is the effect that a new gene may or may not have on the physical or psychological state of the animal that is important. It is this aspect that animal welfare societies need to keep a close eye on, as witnessed by the plight of many dairy cows receiving rBST.

Changes to our food

Although there is some public discussion about the genetic modification of animals, it is the use of GM products in our food that has probably raised the greatest concerns among the public. More than 40 different GM crops have been approved for use in food in the USA. But in the EU only three products – GM soybean, **maize** and tomato paste – have been approved for sale and no new GM crops have been approved by the EU since April 1998. So how are these products used and what are the concerns?

Processed foods

Most processed foods contain ingredients derived from plants such as soybean, maize, oil-seed rape and sugar beet. There are GM varieties of all of these plants. Soybean is high in **protein** so it is used in high-protein animal feed and foods for humans. It is added to food as a binding agent, stabilizer and emulsifier. Binding agents make the different ingredients stick together and emulsifiers prevent the separation of oils and water in food such as a sauce or margarine. In fact, soybean-based ingredients are found in more than 60 per cent of processed foods, including bread, biscuits, baby milk, cereals, margarine, soups, pasta, pizza, ready meals, meat products, flour, sweets, ice-cream, crisps, chocolate, soy sauce, veggie-burgers, tofu, soya milk and pet foods. Soya oil and rape-seed oil used in foods may be labelled as 'vegetable fats' or hydrogenated fats'. Soya oil can be processed to make lecithin. Lecithin binds water and fat together and is used as a thickening agent in milkshakes, biscuits and chocolate bars. The first commercial harvest of GM soybeans in the USA occurred in 1996 and it quickly appeared in foods. Now GM varieties make up 63 per cent of the US soybean harvest.

Maize is used in many processed foods as well as bread and cereals. Maize-based ingredients that may appear on food labels include modified starch, cornflour, corn starch, corn oil, corn syrup, dextrose, glucose and polenta. Maize is also used in animal feed. GM maize is grown commercially in the USA, where it currently makes up 25 per cent of the total crop.

Supermarket shelves are filled with a great range of convenient processed foods. More than half of these foods contain soybean or maize.

Rape-seed oil is widely used in vegetable oil, margarine, oven-ready chips, tinned foods, processed foods, crisps and other snack foods. Although it is found in food in North America, it has not been approved for sale in the EU. It is possible that foods imported from North America could contain GM rape-seed oil. Sugar comes from sugar beet and sugar cane, both of which have GM varieties under trial. It is likely that GM sugar beet will soon be grown in China and South Africa. GM sugar would be used in processed foods such as cakes and biscuits.

Tastier tomatoes

The flavour and shelf life of tomatoes has been improved in recent years by the use of genetic modification. One of the effects of slowing down the ripening time (see page 24) has been the retention of pectin within the tomato. The higher levels of pectin give the product an attractive, glossy appearance and make it easier for food manufacturers to produce the thickness needed in sauces, ketchups and purées. Tomato purées are produced by mashing the tomatoes into a pulp to remove the juice. The aim is to extract the maximum amount of juice with the minimum of processing. The modified tomatoes contain less water and this means that less heat is needed to evaporate the water during processing. Less heat treatment means there is better retention of natural flavours. A GM tomato paste has been approved for sale in the EU, but not the tomatoes themselves.

Fungal 'factories'

Many fungi produce **enzymes** that are useful in food processing. These fungi are grown on a commercial scale to produce industrial quantities of enzyme. The enzymes are used for processing fruit and vegetables, clarifying fruit juice, extracting coffee and spices, and producing sweeteners. Some fungi are now being genetically modified to improve their enzyme-secreting capacity and to produce new enzymes.

> 'GM crops are the same as non-GM crops except for one or two **genes** out of 50,000–70,000 genes already present in nature. For this reason, there is no justification for categorizing them in the same way as highly active drugs.'
>
> Clive Rainbird, AgrEvo (leading **biotechnology** company involved with producing GM crops)

The approval process

When introducing any new technology, including gene technology, into the food chain, it is essential to put in place appropriate safeguards to protect human health. Most countries have laws that require foods containing GM products to be subjected to an extensive range of analytical tests for food safety evaluation before they can be approved for sale. In the EU, these foods have to be assessed by specialist scientific committees in member countries, for example, the UK's Advisory Committee on Novel Foods and Processes. Australia and New Zealand also have a joint food authority, ANZFA, which develops food standards and carries out assessments to ensure the safety of food. These countries have controls in place, not because safety problems have been identified but because they have a lack of familiarity with GM products. These products have only been consumed for a few years. The first indications from North America, where millions of people have eaten GM foods, is that these foods are safe – but nobody knows if there are any long-term effects from eating them.

Animal or vegetable?

Many vegetarians are concerned that genes are being taken from animals and inserted into plants. Scientists are working on a project to insert a fish gene into a potato to give it frost **resistance**. Vegetarians argue that it is wrong to insert animal genes into a vegetable and that the presence of the animal gene changes the food so it can no longer be classed as a vegetable. Others respond that the **DNA** of most organisms is very similar and that the few differences made are unimportant. In fact, the majority of DNA is common to all organisms and only a tiny percentage, albeit a critical percentage, is different – and this is what creates the different species.

The arrival of the first foods containing GM ingredients in Europe caused numerous demonstrations. Protestors gathered outside supermarkets and asked shoppers to sign petitions against the sale of GM foods.

Food tests

Most food tests are based on the concept of substantial equivalence. A new GM food or ingredient is compared with an existing non-GM version of the food. The tests compare the composition, nutritional properties, **allergen** content, and amount of the food that is consumed as well as the type of processing that the food might undergo. If the new food or ingredient is considered to be substantially equivalent to an existing food or ingredient, it can be treated in the same manner with respect to safety and nutrition. This means it can be approved for use. If any differences are identified, the food has to be subjected to extensive animal feeding and toxicological (poison) tests before approval can be given.

However, the definition of substantial equivalence varies from country to country. In the USA and Canada, the presence of new DNA and/or protein does not stop a GM food from being considered substantially equivalent to a conventional food. However, a slightly different definition is used in Europe. In Europe, only highly processed foods derived from GM crops, such as refined oil, white sugar and starch, are considered substantially equivalent to their conventional counterparts. This is because there is no DNA or protein left after processing. During processing, the plants are treated in such a way so as to separate the cellular bits from the oil, sugar or starch. All other ingredients derived from GM crops, such as flour and protein extracts, require a full safety evaluation as they may contain new DNA and/or protein, in either intact or broken-down form. Thus, lecithin from GM soybean would be considered substantially equivalent to conventional lecithin in North America, but not in Europe.

Testing new proteins in food

When genes from an unrelated species are inserted into a food crop, there is a risk that the proteins produced by the new gene will be **toxic** or cause an allergic reaction in people who eat the food. The new proteins would not normally be found in the food – for example the protein produced by the Bt gene (see page 48) is found in bacteria and not in crops.

Scientists carry out a series of laboratory tests, feeding mice with a high dose of the protein, to check that it is not toxic. The new protein is analysed for the presence of any of the 500 combinations of **amino acids** in proteins that are known to trigger an allergic reaction. If they are discovered, the new food crop is abandoned. Finally, the new protein has to be easily digested by the body. Often allergens are difficult to digest and they remain in the gut for longer periods of time and cause a reaction. Scientists test the proteins in the laboratory for their digestibility.

There are concerns that the new protein could react with the plant's own proteins and alter the plant itself. For example, there is a tomato which contains a new gene that produces a protein that makes the tomato taste far sweeter. This could change the nutritional composition of the food. So the new food is analysed at the molecular level to make sure there are no harmful changes.

No amount of testing can insure that GM foods are completely safe. However, the traditional **selective breeding** of new crops is no less risky. Plant breeders take two plants and cross them, combining genes in a completely random manner. This can go wrong. During the 1970s researchers crossed two varieties of potato to produce a potato with greater insect resistance. Unfortunately the new potato had a gene that produced a large amount of a toxic protein that made people ill.

In 2000, starlink corn, a GM crop with protection against the corn borer, was withdrawn from sale. It had been approved for livestock consumption only, but some of the corn **contaminated** other corn that was destined for human consumption. A few people eating contaminated taco shells reported having an allergic reaction. Investigations are underway to see if the new protein Cry9C, produced by genetic engineering, causes allergies.

Labelling

In the USA, GM foods are not treated any differently to natural foods. Therefore there is no requirement for food manufacturers to label their foods as containing GM ingredients. In contrast, GM foods are highly regulated in the EU. There are legal regulations that make sure foodstuffs are specifically labelled when detectable levels of DNA and/or protein derived from genetic modification are present. Food producers and retailers have to include the phrase 'produced from genetically modified soybean' or 'produced from genetically modified maize', as appropriate, on the label. A similar legal requirement exists in Australia.

Testing the DNA

Until the early 1990s there were no reliable analytical methods that enabled scientists to determine whether a food or food ingredient had been genetically modified. Now there is a test based on the polymerase chain reaction, or PCR. This test takes tiny quantities of DNA and replicates, or copies, the DNA billions of times to produce enough DNA for analysis. This technique is also used in forensic science, when pathologists take tiny samples of DNA from crime scenes. Many laboratories are already using this method to detect foods that contain GM ingredients or components.

INGREDIENTS:
Wheat Flour, Margarine (with Emulsifiers: Mono-and Di-Glycer
Fatty Acids, Lecithin; Citric Acid), Water, Reconstituted Whole Mi
Powder, Quorn® Myco-Protein Product (Myco-Protein; Egg Album
Flavourings), Mushrooms, Vegetable Oil and Hydrogenated Vegeta
Oil, Whipping Cream, Onion, White Wine, Modified Starch, Salt,
Lactose, Dried Herbs, Milk Protein, Hydrolysed Vegetable Protein*,
Spices, Raising Agents (Sodium Diphosphate, Sodium Bicarbonate),
Maize Starch, Flavourings, Mushroom Powder, Sugar, Yeast Extract,
Vegetable Extract, Flour Treatment Agent (L-Cysteine Hydrochloride).
*Produced from genetically modified soya.

WARNING:
This product may contain traces of nuts.

STORAGE INSTRUCTIONS:
Keep frozen and use within the following periods:

In the European Union, foods containing GM ingredients must be clearly labelled as such. These tortilla chips contain GM maize.

There are problems with labelling however. There is no single test that can be used to detect all types of GM material. Also, there is no international agreement relating to the labelling of GM foods. Even the countries that require labelling do not have the same rules. For example, they vary on the amount of GM protein or DNA that can be present in a food before it has to be labelled as containing a GM ingredient. Nor is there any agreement on how the GM foods should be analysed.

Furthermore, GM and non-GM crops can become mixed together during harvest, transportation, processing and storage. It is relatively easy for a non-GM product to be contaminated with small amounts of a GM product without the suppliers being aware of the fact. A system to separate the GM and non-GM products at various stages of processing needs to be set up and maintained.

Should GM foods be labelled?

There has been considerable debate over the issue of labelling. Food manufacturers claim that GM ingredients are no different to natural ones. For example, pure starch from GM maize is identical to starch from non-GM maize. When some foods are processed the DNA is broken down or removed so it is impossible to test whether that food ingredient came from a GM source. Opposing this view are the consumers who want to know the origin of all the ingredients. Many consumers are not concerned that GM ingredients may be used in foods, but they would like clear, unambiguous labelling to help them make informed choices. They may decide that any potential risk is small and buy the food, or decide to avoid it. Either way, they want to have the information in order to make a choice. It is possible that some producers will be able to label their foods as GM-free. However, they would have to be able to support their claim with analytical laboratory results.

'These are the toughest GM licensing laws in the world. With this vote, consumers can have confidence that GM products licensed for sale in the EU have met the toughest standards anywhere.'

David Bowe, Labour MEP, commenting on the new EU rules controlling GM licensing

GM and the environment

GM crops are developed under carefully controlled laboratory and glasshouse conditions. However, once a new or modified plant has been produced, it is likely to be grown outside. Scientists have to determine the risk to the environment and to native species before the crops can be planted commercially.

Genetic pollution

Once GM crops are planted outside, there is little to stop these plants crossing with wild plants growing locally. This is referred to as genetic pollution. Some scientists predict that, within just one year, a significant number of weeds growing close to a GM crop with herbicide **resistance** could have acquired this **gene**. The result could be super-weeds that would be more difficult to kill using traditional herbicides. Some plants can cross with other plants more easily than others. For example, oil-seed rape is a crop grown for oil that was produced by crossing two species of cabbage. It is the most likely of all GM crops to cross with non-GM plants.

This crop of non-GM oil-seed rape has been planted quite close to another field of the same crop. If this was a GM oil-seed rape crop, the two fields would have to be 400 metres apart.

Flowers need to be **pollinated** before they can set seed. Some plants are self-pollinated, that is, their own pollen pollinates and **fertilizes** their own eggs. Other plants require cross-pollination. The pollen is carried by wind, water or an animal from a flower on one plant to a flower on another plant. Oil-seed rape produces large quantities of pollen and attracts many pollinating insects. Recent crop trials in the UK have found that pollen from GM oil-seed rape pollinated non-GM oil-seed rape growing more than 400 metres away and 7 per cent of the resulting seed was herbicide resistant.

Avoiding genetic pollution

It is impossible to stop pollen being carried away from GM crops. But, there are ways of minimizing the spread. One is the presence of a buffer zone between GM plants and non-GM plants. The buffer zone is used to grow non-GM plants of the same type, which are harvested and then destroyed at the end of the growing season. In the UK it is recommended that GM oil-seed rape is planted not less than 400 metres from the nearest non-GM oil-seed rape, and that the GM plants are surrounded by a 6-metre crop of non-GM oil-seed rape, to trap some of the pollen.

The pollen problem can be avoided in some GM crops, such as sugar beet, by harvesting before the flowers are produced. There are trees that have been genetically modified so that they are more easily pulped and made into paper. These trees take some years to mature and will be harvested before they start to produce flowers. However, this is not possible with cereals, soybean and oil-seed rape, as it is the seeds and/or fruits that are harvested.

Risk assessment

Before a GM crop is planted it is important that a risk assessment is carried out. The risks may vary from country to country. For example, in the future the tropical crop cassava may be genetically modified. The risks of genetic pollution in South America, where there are wild varieties of cassava, are much greater than if the crop was planted in Africa, where there is no wild species and so no risk of cross-pollination.

> 'There should be no release of GM native plants until it can be guaranteed they cannot cross-pollinate with our wild plants.'
>
> Dr Brian Johnson, **biotechnology** advisor for the conservation group English Nature

Gene protection

The spread of genes into wild species can be prevented by making sure that any seed produced by GM crops cannot **germinate**. This could be achieved using technology called gene protector (GP). GP prevents a seed from germinating. Should there be successful cross-pollination between a GM plant with gene protection and a non-GM plant, any resulting seeds would be unable to germinate. But there is a problem. Worldwide, farmers save seed to sow the next year. Approximately 80 per cent of crops in the developing world are produced from saved seed. This would be impossible with GP crops, as the seeds would not germinate.

During the germination of a wheat seed, the seed coat splits and the young root, called a radicle, emerges. If this seed had gene protection it would be unable to germinate.

Many argue that seeds with GP would be no different to **hybrid** seeds currently on sale. Hybrid seeds are produced by crossing two different varieties of plant to produce a hybrid that is more vigorous or greater yielding than the parents. The farmer does not save the seed from hybrid plants. This is because the seeds produced by a hybrid plant produce plants that usually do not grow as well as their parents. So, farmers have to buy fresh hybrid seeds each year. Just as farmers have a choice over hybrid or non-hybrid seeds, farmers would have a choice of buying GP or non-GP seeds. If they wanted to save seed, they could buy non-GP seeds. During 1999 there was considerable outcry against this technology, especially by developing countries and development agencies, so research has been halted. However, this technology offers a very effective method of protecting native plants from genetic pollution.

Avoiding pesticides

Each year, farmers all over the world apply large quantities of pesticides, herbicides and fungicides to their crops. This has adverse effects on the environment. Some pesticides kill non-target animals and affect whole food chains. Pesticides and herbicides can run off fields into rivers, lakes and streams, where they harm aquatic life. The chemicals, if not used carefully, can harm the farmer. In many parts of the world, farmers do not have the right safety equipment and their health is therefore at risk. Crops are often sprayed many times during the growing season, especially after wet weather, and the spraying is not always effective against pests such as the corn borer, which tunnels deep into the plant.

The new generation of crops that have genetically engineered defences against pests do not have to be sprayed. Farmers growing GM soybean in the US report that they are using less pesticide. They are using one type, rather than two or three different ones, and they are not having to use the more powerful ones. Their costs have fallen, in some cases by as much as 50 per cent. Soybean supplies are now 16 per cent cheaper and this has reduced costs of processed foods in US shops.

GM crops with resistance to nematodes (tiny worm-like animals found in the soil) could significantly reduce the use of some of the most toxic and environmentally damaging pesticides in widespread use. Conventional plant breeding has failed to produce effective nematode-resistant varieties, but GM varieties are in development.

Developing resistance

One effect of using repeated applications of the same pesticide is the development of resistance in the pest. Some individuals in a population may have a gene that gives them resistance to the pesticide. This means that they are not killed by the pesticide so they survive and breed. The gene for resistance is passed to the next generation. Their offspring survive too and breed. The gene quickly spreads through the whole population. The same thing would happen when GM crops with pest resistance are planted for a number of years. Not all of the pests eating the plants will be killed by the built-in pesticide. The only way to overcome the problem is to develop new pesticides to which the pests have no resistance.

More birds

GM crops have been grown in the US for more than six years. Far fewer pesticides are now sprayed on to farmland and this has lead to more insects feeding in and around the fields. This in turn provides food for insect-eating birds. The numbers of these birds has increased, especially finches, pheasants and quails. Birds of prey, such as owls and hawks are increasing too, because there are more small birds for them to feed on. However, these changes in bird life could be due to other changes in farm practice. Insects could be encouraged by farmers spreading a mulch (layer of straw or matting) over the soil to help retain moisture.

'There is a trend emerging that shows biotech crops, especially cotton, significantly reduce the amount of chemical insecticides that must be sprayed to control insect pests.'

Dr Kalaitzandonakes, Associate Professor of Agribusiness, University of Missouri

Pests can reduce cotton yields considerably. To prevent this damage, farmers have to spray their crops regularly during the growing season.

Herbicide resistance

Vast quantities of herbicides are used each year to control the weeds growing in fields of crops. Farmers often use herbicides that persist in the ground for several weeks to kill any weeds and stop new ones from germinating. These herbicides are designed to kill one particular group of weeds – for example some herbicides kill only weeds with broad leaves, leaving narrow-leaved cereal crops such as wheat and **maize** unharmed. Although the cereal crops are tolerant of the herbicide, there can be a temporary slow-down in growth. In addition, these chemicals can kill worms and other soil animals.

The new GM crops with their in-built resistance to herbicides may allow more effective weed control. The glyphosate-resistant crops (see page 26) can be safely sprayed with glyphosate herbicides. GM crops are sown straight into undisturbed soil. The farmers don't have to spray the ground before or after sowing. They can leave the weeds for a while and then spray once to kill them all. This allows insects and birds to feed on the flowers and seeds of the weeds. Once killed, the dead weeds form a mulch on the ground and this helps to reduce water loss from the soil. It also helps to stop more weeds from growing.

'Because Bt corn is so effective in controlling corn borers, there is concern that resistance to Bt could develop quite rapidly [in corn borers] unless appropriate non-Bt corn refuge plantings are employed to maintain a susceptible population of corn borers.'
Randy Higgins, Kansas State University biologist

Weeds and birds

Some conservation organizations, both in the UK and USA, are concerned that if too many weeds and pests are killed it could result in less food for insects and the birds that depend on them, especially the corn bunting, partridge and the skylark. For example, most of the UK's traditional meadows have been lost and birds and insects have become far more dependent on weeds for food. As many as 20 different kinds of weeds may grow around a field, providing food to many insects and birds. Although farmers use fewer herbicides on GM crops, they can apply a single large dose for maximum weed control. Recent crop trials of GM sugar beet have found that more insects were found in these fields than in fields of conventional sugar beet. The GM sugar beet only had to be sprayed with glyphosate twice, while conventional crops received up to eight sprays of a selective herbicide. The weeds were found to attract the pests away from the GM plants while the dead weeds provided a habitat for other insects. Overall, biodiversity was greater in the GM sugar beet fields.

Putting useful insects at risk

GM crops with the Bt gene contain a **toxin** that kills insect larvae that eat the leaves or seeds. The larvae do not die immediately. Instead they stop eating and die a few days later. During this time they could be eaten by other animals. There is a chance that insects beneficial to the crop could be harmed by feeding on poisoned larvae too, for example lacewings, ladybirds and butterfly larvae. Only now are research teams looking at this potential threat to insects, both in the laboratory and in the field. Unfortunately, the initial results have been confusing and in some cases contradictory.

Scientists from the Swiss Federal Research Station for Agroecology and Agriculture studied lacewings that feed on the European corn borer. There is a variety of GM maize with the Bt gene to protect against the corn borer. The researchers found that lacewings which had eaten core borers raised on GM maize had a higher death rate than the lacewings feeding on corn borers that had been raised on non GM maize.

Scientists from the Scottish Crop Research Institute found that ladybirds fed aphids which had been eating a variety of GM potato did not live as long as ladybirds fed aphids from ordinary potatoes. Also, they did not produce as many eggs. However, another group has found that ladybirds are unaffected when they eat insects that have been reared on GM crops.

Aphids suck the juices from plant stems and reduce crop yields. Their natural predator is the ladybird. Both the adult and larval ladybird eat aphids. Some insecticides used to control the aphids can kill the ladybirds too.

The colourful monarch butterfly is at the centre of controversy. Some researchers believe that its caterpillars could be harmed by eating pollen from GM maize, while others claim that there is no risk at all.

There is concern that the North American monarch butterfly could be harmed by GM maize with the Bt gene. Monarch butterfly caterpillars feed on milkweed, a weed that is often found growing near maize fields. When the maize is in flower, large quantities of pollen cover the leaves of the milkweed, and when the caterpillars eat the leaves, they eat the pollen at the same time. Experiments have found that monarch caterpillars die within days of eating the pollen of GM maize. Recently, one of the most powerful versions of Bt maize has been withdrawn from sale. This variety, known as 'event-176', produced up to 40 times more toxin than some other varieties. The other varieties appear not to harm the butterfly larvae.

'There's no doubt that there is potential for harm both in terms of human safety and in the diversity of our environment from GM foods or crops.'

Tony Blair, the British Prime Minister

Back to organic

Historically, farming was all 'organic'. Farmers used a few natural pesticides and organic **fertilizers** in the form of compost, sewage and manure. After World War II, the introduction of chemical fertilizers and pesticides led to more intensive agriculture – larger fields, more machinery and higher yields. Hedgerows were ripped up and meadows were ploughed to create large fields that were more suited to the large machinery. In recent years, the decline of wildlife and the effect of indiscriminate use of pesticides and fertilizers on the environment have led to a growing interest in organic farming, where the farmers use no chemicals or **antibiotics**. The recent food scares and bad press given to GM crops has resulted in more people buying organic foods. UK supermarkets report a 40 per cent increase in organic sales.

Organic farming does not use chemicals such as herbicides and pesticides. This means that crop yields can be lower as a result of there being more weeds and pest damage.

The planting of GM crops threatens organic farming. Current organic standards in Europe do not permit organic food to contain any GM ingredients. If GM crops are grown close to organic crops there is a potential for cross-pollination causing the organic crop to become **contaminated**. Scientific reports indicate that GM contamination is inevitable and organic producers would have to be allowed to have a set level of contamination and still qualify as organic. Foods that claim to be GM-free would need to be tested to prove that they do not contain any foreign **DNA**.

A sustainable approach

All farming has some impact on the environment. Intensive agriculture has high productivity levels, but at the expense of the environment. Organic farming has less environmental impact but, generally, lower productivity. One sustainable solution will probably involve a combined GM-organic approach. A sustainable system would be one that could be carried out for many years without damaging the environment. It could still include high productivity – a necessity given the rapidly increasing world population. For example, the area under cultivation of the tropical crop cassava has increased by 43 per cent since 1970. This is an unsustainable increase because it has resulted in the loss of valuable tropical ecosystems, such as rainforest and grassland. The introduction of a GM variety of cassava with built-in pest protection could increase the yield of the harvest and reduce the need to cultivate more land.

Cassava is a staple food for 600 million people. The average yield is between 7 and 8 tonnes per hectare, but with pest and disease control the yield could rise to 80 tonnes. This could be achieved using GM varieties.

The future of GM food

Over the next few years, a wide range of genetically modified plants will come on the market, some of which could have a significant effect on agriculture and our diets.

Self-fertilizing crops

One line of research that has great promise involves giving crops such as cereals the ability to produce their own **fertilizer**. Nitrogen in the form of nitrate is an essential nutrient for plants. Farmers apply nitrogen fertilizers to their crops to ensure that they grow well. Plants of the pea family do not require such fertilizers as they have bacteria living in their roots that take nitrogen gas from the air and convert it into a form of nitrogen that the plant can use. Scientists have located the nitrogen-fixing **gene** in bacteria and are attempting to insert it into wheat plants. This is still in the experimental stage, but if successful it could lead to dramatic reduction in fertilizer use, which would benefit both farmers and the environment.

Healthy foods

There are a number of diseases that are caused by a lack of certain minerals and vitamins in the diet. For example, anaemia (lack of iron in the blood) is common in Asia, where people eat a lot of white rice which provides little iron. A new type of genetically modified rice has been produced that has three times the normal level of iron. This means that a person eating a portion of the rice would get up to half their daily iron requirement. Every year in the developing world millions of people suffer from blindness as a result of a vitamin A deficiency. A new GM rice with a high level of vitamin A could eliminate this problem.

'To dream of equal distribution of money or food resources worldwide is a nice dream, but it can never be achieved... The only solution is to build in vitamin A into their basic food and that's exactly what we are doing for 2.4 billion people and I hope that people who are so far extremely sceptical of this new technique will see that here is an example where this technique has been used for something beneficial to the consumer.'
Professor Ingo Potrykus, of the Swiss Federal Institute of Technology, who has developed a GM rice with a high concentration of vitamin A that is currently undergoing tests

Many people in the developing world could have much improved diets simply by eating GM rice with a more nutritious content.

In the future, we could be offered a whole range of 'health' foods, such as tomatoes with increased vitamin content, non-allergenic peanuts, wheat with increased levels of folic acid to prevent the disabling disorder spina bifida and wheat with increased fibre to reduce the risk of colon cancer.

Will the public ever accept GM foods?

GM foods in Europe have received a very bad press, and photographs of people destroying GM crop trials and demonstrating outside supermarkets have appeared in newspapers. Today, despite the fact that three GM foods are approved for sale in the EU, there are very few GM products in the shops. This contrasts greatly with North America, where a wide range of GM foods are on sale. All the evidence indicates that these foods are safe to eat. However, recent scares related to the production of food in Europe – including **BSE** in cattle and foods **contaminated** with **dioxin** – have made the public wary of new foods that might put their health at risk. In addition, the environmental effects have still to be determined – another issue that concerns the European public. Europeans will need a lot of convincing before the GM foods will be accepted. Meanwhile, the sales of organic foods are rising dramatically and outstripping supply.

Designer oils

Oil-crops, such as linseed and oil-seed rape, are important sources of vegetable oil for the food, pharmaceutical (drug) and cosmetic industries. But they could become far more important in the future as supplies of oil and gas start to run out. These oil-producing plants could be genetically modified to produce oils that were originally obtained from fossil fuel oil. The gene responsible for making a particular oil would be located in another organism, such as a bacterium or plant, removed and inserted into the **DNA** of a crop plant. For example, the coriander plant produces petroselinic acid, a compound used in the oil industry. The gene could be identified and removed and inserted into oil-seed rape. As much as one-third of European farmland is no longer used to grow crops. This land could be used to grow more oil crops.

Oil-seed rape could be modified to produce specific types of oils that could be used by pharmaceutical and cosmetic companies.

Biodiversity

Over the last 60 years, more than three-quarters of the world's food plant varieties have vanished as farmers have concentrated on a few commercial strains. In Europe, seed producers have to pay a licence fee for every variety of seed that they sell. This has meant that they have stopped selling many of the less popular varieties on economic grounds. Once a plant variety is dropped from the seed lists, it can disappear completely, unless it is cultivated by conservation societies.

Agriculture is becoming increasingly dependent on a small range of crops. For example, in 1900 there were more than 30,000 different varieties of rice. Today, only a fraction of this number are still in cultivation. Many useful varieties with natural **resistance** to pests and disease have been lost. In some countries, a single type of crop

Research institutes are looking to improve less well known crop plants such as the wing bean.

or crop variety is grown over a large area. This is called monoculture. These huge fields of a single crop are far more vulnerable to disease and pests than fields where the crops are more varied. It is likely that if the GM crops are successful, they too could be planted over large areas. It could be dangerous to depend on a small range of crops. Climatic change and the appearance of new diseases and pests could wipe out certain varieties of crops.

HRH Prince of Wales

One of the most outspoken critics of GM crops is HRH the Prince of Wales. In June 1999 he published a list of ten questions and answers about GM crops and their threat to farming and the countryside – for example, 'Do we need GM food in this country', 'Is GM food safe for us to eat?', 'What effect will GM crops have on the world's poorest countries?' Many people did not agree with his views, especially his very negative attitude to science. However, his comments attracted a lot of attention and as a result the issues were debated in the public domain.

Conclusion

The world's population stands at 6 billion, of whom 800 million in the developing world are starving. In a few decades the world's population will have doubled, with most of the increase occurring in the poorest parts of the world. Somehow we have to find ways of feeding all these extra people. There needs to be a 70 per cent increase in the production of rice by 2025 just to keep up with demand. Some argue that there is plenty of food – it just needs to be distributed more fairly. This ideal would require a drastic change in world politics and economic attitudes. As this is unlikely, people have to look for other ways, especially advances in agriculture and food technology.

In the developing world, many farmers grow crops such as sorghum, millet and cassava and they cannot afford fertilizers and pesticides. They need GM varieties of their crops that will give greater yields.

Helping subsistence farmers

The producers of the new GM crops claim that their plants, due to their greater **resistance** to disease and pests, will lead to higher productivity. The plants also require fewer **fertilizers** and pesticides, so wildlife benefits. Some of the new crops being developed will be able to grow on marginal land where current varieties will not grow – for example, land that has been damaged by salt water after flooding. However, the first generation of GM crops are mostly aimed at developed countries, where there are economic benefits in reducing the costs of fertilizer and pesticide use. The commercial companies have targeted economic crops such as **maize**, soybean, cotton, rubber and papaya, for which there will be a financial return.

However, most of the developing world rely on staple crops such as plantain, cassava, sorghum and millet, which are grown by **subsistence farmers** who cannot afford fertilizer and pesticides. These crops have proved difficult to improve by conventional breeding and they suffer from numerous diseases and pests. But they have been ignored by the commercial companies because they offer no return. Consequently, the productivity of these crops has increased by just 3 per cent over the last 30 years. In contrast, wheat has increased by 130 per cent. Just doubling the current yields would have a significant impact on the food supply. **Biotechnology** will not feed the world unless its benefits reach these farmers.

The use of GM technology in food production is still new. Nobody knows whether the consumption of these foods will be harmful in the long term or whether there will be any effects on the environment or on biodiversity. What is important is that the new technology is developed with care and that safety is considered at all stages. It is important that developments in agriculture and food technology are not left solely to commercial companies. They must be monitored by governments and international agencies, who need to evaluate the threats and benefits of GM to people both in developed and developing countries, and to propose a suitable framework for the future.

'I think we have to consider, whether we like it or not, that genetic engineering may actually have some solutions, if we look at it sensibly.'
Sir John Beringer, Dean of Science at Bristol University, former chairman of the UK government's advisory committee on releases into the environment

'As for most complex issues there is no single simple remedy. Biotechnology is not a panacea [solution] for world hunger. However, when combined with traditional breeding, good agricultural practice and sound economic policies, it can be an important factor in achieving improved standards of health and economic security for all the world's people.'
Nigel J. Taylor and Claude M. Fauquet, ILTAB / Donald Danforth Plant Science Center, University of Missouri

Timeline

1859   Charles Darwin publishes *The Origin of Species* in which he describes the process by which living organisms could have changed and evolved over time by means of natural selection.

1860s   **Chromosomes** are seen in dividing cells, but the term 'chromosome' is not used until 1888. The word means 'coloured bodies' and was applied because these structures or 'bodies' took up coloured dyes when the cell was stained. Gregor Mendel completes his genetic experiments with pea plants and produces a set of laws of inheritance that form the basis of modern genetics.

1871   Nucleic acid is first discovered in the sperm of trout but is not identified.

1879   Walter Fleming discovers mitosis (division of the **nucleus**) but does not report his findings until 1882.

1880s   The American scientist August Weismann suggests that the sex cells of animals possess something which is passed from generation to generation. He theorizes that each new cell receives half the material from the parent nucleus.

1909   The British biologist William Bateson first uses the term 'genetics'.

1920s   **DNA** is first identified and analysed.

1940s   George Beadle and Edward Tatum, working with bread mould in the USA, show that one **gene** is responsible for one **enzyme**.

1950   Maurice Wilkins and Rosalind Franklin use X-rays to show that DNA is arranged in a helix.

1953   Francis Crick and James Watson publish their proposed structure of DNA.

1956 –59   Francois Jacob and Jacques Monod determine the mechanism by which genes are switched on and off.

1961   Francis Crick, Sydney Brenner and RJ Watts-Tobin publish their theory of the **genetic code**.

1962   Francis Crick, James Watson and Maurice Wilkins are awarded the Nobel Prize for Medicine.

1970   Hamilton Smith at Johns Hopkins University in Baltimore USA isolates the first restriction enzyme using a bacterium. Restriction enzymes are the 'molecular scissors' that cut DNA in specific places.

1972   Janet Mertz and Ron Davis at Stanford University, California USA produce the first **recombinant DNA** using restriction enzymes.

1973   Stanley Cohen and Herbert Boyer use restriction enzymes to successfully transfer genes from one species to another.

1977   First recombinant DNA containing mammalian DNA is produced.

1980   First **transgenic** mouse is born.
        At the University of Ghent in Belgium, Professor Van Montagu demonstrates that a soil bacterium called *Agrobacterium* inserts its own DNA into the DNA of the plant from which it feeds, transforming the genetic structure of the plant.

1983   The Mexican scientist Luis Herrera-Estrella uses *Agrobacterium* to transfer an **antibiotic resistance** gene into a tobacco plant and in doing so becomes the first person to create an artificially, genetically modified plant.
        Kary Mullis invents the method of polymerase chain reaction (PCR) to make copies of DNA fragments.

1987   The Monsanto corporation announces that it has finally succeeded in engineering the first artificially insect-resistant crop plant, using a gene from a bacterium which is naturally insect resistant.

1990   Professor Don Grierson, of the University of Nottingham, removes a gene from a tomato, reverses it and places it back into the tomato. This change makes the tomato ripen more slowly and stay fresh for longer.
        First GMO – a modified yeast for bread making – is used in food.

1993   GM tomatoes go on sale in the USA.

1996   First GM soybean and **maize** crops are planted in North America.
        Dolly the sheep, the first **clone** of an adult mammalian cell, is born.

1997   GM food goes on sale in Europe although not labelled as such.

1999   Protestors destroy GM crop trials in Europe.

2000   Monsanto offers the technology for vitamin A enriched rice for free to improve nutrition in developing countries.

2001   Researchers at the **biotechnology** company Syngenta publish a draft of the rice **genome**.
        Euro-MPs vote in favour of tough rules to test and monitor the safety of GM food and crops.

Glossary

allergen protein that produces allergic responses, for example proteins found on grass pollen, cat fur and certain foods

allergy extreme sensitivity to a substance, for example nuts or grass pollen, causing the body to react when it comes into contact with it

amino acids building blocks of proteins. Proteins are made up of a chain of amino acids joined together. There are 20 naturally occurring amino acids, including eight so-called essential amino acids, which cannot be made by the adult human body and have to be obtained in the diet.

antibiotic drug that kills or inhibits the growth of harmful bacteria. As antibiotics are used more widely, bacteria are becoming resistant to these drugs.

biotechnology use of biological processes in industry and medicine; for example, the use of genetically engineered bacteria to produce drugs

BSE (also called mad cow disease) fatal disease affecting cattle that centres on the brain

chromosome one of the thread-like structures in a nucleus, made up of DNA and protein. Each chromosome carries many different genes. There are 23 pairs of chromosomes in a human cell, except in the sex cells which have 23 chromosomes and in red blood cells which have no chromosomes.

clone an individual that is genetically identical to one or more other individuals

contamination presence of a pollutant or infection agent

cytoplasm 'jelly-like' contents of a cell, minus the nucleus, where proteins are made

dioxin highly toxic compound that is a by-product of some industrial processes

DNA (deoxyribonucleic acid) substance in all living things that carries the genetic code, found in the nucleus

embryo term for an egg after it has been fertilized, when it is in its early stages of development

enzyme protein produced by cells that is able to make possible or catalyse (increase the speed of) reactions within living organisms

fertilization joining together of a male and female sex cell to form a new individual

fertilizer chemicals or natural substances, such as manure, which are rich in nutrients and are added to soil to increase its fertility

gene unit of inheritance that is passed on from parent to offspring, made up of a length of DNA on a chromosome

genetic code sequence of chemical bases in DNA that code for specific amino acids

genome all the DNA sequences contained in the chromosomes of an organism

germinate when a seed starts to grow (producing a shoot and root)

growth medium solution (containing nutrients) on which organisms such as bacteria are grown

hybrid the offspring of two plants or animals of different varieties or species. Often hybrids are healthier and more vigorous than their parents.

maize (also called corn) cereal crop that produces seeds that are used in many processed foods

malnutrition illness caused by a diet that lacks sufficient nutrients such as vitamins and minerals

molecule two or more atoms bonded together

mutant individual that has undergone genetic change that may or may not be beneficial

nucleus dense structure within a cell, surrounded by a membrane, that contains the DNA

pollinate when pollen is transferred from the anthers (male reproductive part) of one flower to the stigma (female reproductive part) of another

propagated when plants are reproduced from the parent stock, for example by taking cuttings

protein large molecule made from small units called amino acids. Proteins are important for growth and repair and have many functions in the body.

recombinant DNA DNA made up of DNA from different sources that has been joined together

resistance ability of an organism to tolerate something. For example, a bacterium carrying resistance to a particular antibiotic cannot be killed by that type of antibiotic.

RNA (ribonucleic acid) similar to DNA but has a single strand. Found in the nucleus and cytoplasm where it is involved in the synthesis of protein.

selective breeding choosing individual plants or animals with desired characteristics and interbreeding them to produce a new strain of the particular organism

subsistence farmer someone who farms a small plot of land that just provides their family with food and does not supply a surplus that can be sold

toxin (toxic) poison produced by a living organism (poisonous)

transgenic term describing an organism containing genetic material that has been artificially inserted from another species

United Nations (UN) association of the world's nations, established in 1942, with headquarters in New York. It was originally set up as a peace-seeking organization, but now there are many UN agencies involved with global issues such as food and health.

Sources of information

Further reading

Scientifically Engineered Foods: The Debate over What's on Your Plate, Allan B Cobb (Rosen Publishing Group, 2000)
High-Tech Harvest: A Look at Genetically Engineered Foods, Elizabeth L Marshall (Franklin Watts, 1999)
Genetic Engineering – The Facts, Sally Morgan (Evans Brothers, 2001)
The Engineer in the Garden, Colin Tudge (Pimlico, 1995)

Websites

There are many websites displaying information about GM foods, including those of governments, biotechnology companies and campaigning organizations. But beware – the information they hold is not always completely accurate.
www.ncbe.reading.ac.uk/NCBE/GMFOOD/main.html
This site, run by NCBE at Reading University, is a good place to start. The centre is concerned with promoting biotechnology education, helping young people to understand the technology, how it is applied and regulated, and to assist informed debate about the issues. As well as providing accurate and accessible information it has links to the

most important GM food sites on the Internet, including those of governments, companies, organizations, research institutes and the media.

www.aventis.com

www.monsanto.com and www.monsanto.co.uk

These websites belong to the leading biotechnology companies involved with the genetic modification of crops, and they provide information on their research. In addition, the Monsanto site hosts a biotechnology information centre.

www.defra.gov.uk

This is the website of the UK government's Department of Environment, Farming and Rural Affairs (DEFRA). It has information on GM crops trials in the UK.

www.usda.gov

www.fda.gov

www.epa.gov

These are the websites of the US-based government departments involved with GM crops.

www.health.gov.au

The Australian government's Department of Health site includes information on the safety of food.

www.greenpeace.com

www.foe.org.uk

Greenpeace and Friends of the Earth are two of the leading environmental campaigning organizations very concerned about the development of GM crops.

www.nuffieldfoundation.org/bioethics

The Nuffield Council of Bioethics set up a working party to study the issues associated with GM crops. They concluded that the application of genetic modification to crops had the potential to bring about significant benefits such as improved nutrition, enhanced pest resistance, increased yields and new products such as vaccines. They recommended a major increase in financial support for GM crop research together with the implementation of international safe guards. The full text of the report 'Genetically modified crops: the ethical and social issues' is available on the website.

Author sources

In addition to the websites above, the author used the following materials in the writing of this book:

Magazines – *British Medical Journal, Farmer's Weekly, Nature, New Scientist, Science*

Newspapers – *Guardian, Daily Telegraph, The Times*

Index